T0209836

Ornaments of Grace

A Mentoring Bible Study for
Young Married Women

Curriculum based on Titus 2 principles
PARTICIPANT LESSON BOOK

LEISA RESS

WESTBOW
P R E S S®
A DIVISION OF THOMAS NELSON
& ZONDERVAN

ESV: Unless otherwise stated, Scripture quotations are from the ESV® Bible (The Holy Bible, English Standard Version®), copyright © 2001 by Crossway, a publishing ministry of Good News Publishers. Used by permission. All rights reserved.

NIV: Scripture quotations marked (NIV) are taken from the Holy Bible, New International Version®, NIV®. Copyright © 1973, 1978, 1984, 2011 by Biblica, Inc.™ Used by permission of Zondervan. All rights reserved worldwide. www.zondervan.com The "NIV" and "New International Version" are trademarks registered in the United States Patent and Trademark Office by Biblica, Inc.

NLT: Scripture quotations marked (NLT) are taken from the Holy Bible, New Living Translation, copyright ©1996, 2004, 2015 by Tyndale House Foundation. Used by permission of Tyndale House Publishers, Inc., Carol Stream, Illinois 60188. All rights reserved.

Floral and Photo Styling by Nicole Bozell of Blossom and Stem
Cover Photo by Lauren Spillman of Signature Lime Photography

WestBow Press books may be ordered through booksellers or by contacting:

WestBow Press
A Division of Thomas Nelson & Zondervan
1663 Liberty Drive
Bloomington, IN 47403
www.westbowpress.com
1 (866) 928-1240

Because of the dynamic nature of the Internet, any web addresses or links contained in this book may have changed since publication and may no longer be valid. The views expressed in this work are solely those of the author and do not necessarily reflect the views of the publisher, and the publisher hereby disclaims any responsibility for them.

Any people depicted in stock imagery provided by Getty Images are models, and such images are being used for illustrative purposes only.
Certain stock imagery © Getty Images.

ISBN: 978-1-9736-2710-4 (sc)
ISBN: 978-1-9736-2709-8 (e)

Print information available on the last page.

WestBow Press rev. date: 04/26/2018

Proverbs 3:21, 22 (NIV) - ". . . preserve sound judgment and discernment, do not let them out of your sight; they will be life for you, an ornament to grace your neck."

Titus 2:1, 3-5 (ESV) - "But as for you, teach what accords with sound doctrine. Older women likewise are to be reverent in behavior, not slanderers or slaves to much wine. They are to teach what is good, and so train the young women to love their husbands and children, to be self-controlled, pure, working at home, kind and submissive to their own husbands, that the word of God may not be reviled."

Dedication

This book is dedicated with much affection to my husband, Fred Ress, and to my children, Meredith Walton and Evan Ress. Each of them knows enough to disqualify me from writing a book on mentoring, and yet loves me with such grace.

Fred and I are so thankful for the beautiful adults God has led our children to become and for the blessed relationships we enjoy with them and their families. We count their spouses, John Walton and Cassyum Detmer Ress as our children as well. We adore our wonderful grandchildren, Cate, Paul, and Claire Walton. And of course, we love our little grand dogs, Leo and Artie Ress.

Contents

Foreword

By Caroline Gilchrist

I have had the privilege and pleasure of being a part of the *Ornaments of Grace* ministry as it has evolved over a period of several years. It is a ministry that is exciting and rewarding for both the mentors and the women who commit to go through this six-week program. I have been encouraged and impressed by the young women who clearly come seeking the Lord with a desire to follow Him and to try to be good wives and mothers. I have personally experienced the rewards from seeing how God can use older women to share their experiences and pour into younger women. This ministry does not ask for these women to be anything but willing to share their successes and failures, in humility, and share how God has worked in their individual lives.

The beauty and fun of this ministry is that the mentoring process is accomplished through the demonstration, preparation and sharing of meals, followed by discussion of Biblical principles that apply to these women's daily lives at home. The meal preparation is fun, instructive, and adds a creative element to each class. The meal sharing provides an opportunity to develop and foster relationship. The discussion that follows continues to build the relationships and share how God's principles can be woven into our lives. I have been amazed how in just six short weeks, some of the women have expressed that the class has impacted them in a significant way. Some of the relationships continue even after the class is over, as these women have found a loving and willing resource. This does not even take into consideration the rewards that the mentors reap from these young women!

Leisa Ress has been both passionate and persistent in the development and growth of this ministry. She has a love for the mentoring process and has given this her heart. Leisa has not in any way been selfish about this ministry, but has welcomed any and all ideas in her efforts to make it the best that it can be. I have no doubt that it will continue to grow and evolve with her careful shepherding. Leisa may not have initially had the goal for this ministry to multiply (like the loaves and the fishes - how appropriate), but God has clearly led her down this path. It is out of her obedience that this ministry can now be used for a more widespread impact of God's love in young women. We pray that you will be blessed by this ministry and be *Ornaments of Grace*.

Testimonials

As a student, OOG opened my heart to what God had to say about living into womanhood as His disciple and as a steward of family and home. There *are* better ways of being according to God's Word, and *Ornaments* isn't afraid to tread the toes of what society may say about a woman's calling inside and outside the home. As a leader and host, it was my privilege to empower women to get beyond all they may be intimidated by, whether in the kitchen or in the Scriptures. It's no accident that the stomach and heart are close together.

Nicole Bozell – Wife, Mother, Floral Designer
Saved by Grace, Living by Faith

Hebrews 13:2 – "Don't forget to show hospitality to strangers, for some who have done this have entertained angels without realizing it!" Isn't it interesting how certain moments in life tend to surface in the memory? A blessed memory that stands out in my past is hosting missionaries on furlough. These folks who dedicated their lives to spreading the Good News about Jesus have often come as strangers but left as lifelong friends.

Psalm 20:1 – "May the Lord answer you in the day of trouble."
Hosting an *Ornaments of Grace* group of women just a few months after my husband of 50 years left to be with Jesus in Heaven is another happy memory. These wonderful women ministered to me as servants of the Most High God. What a blessing and joy to entertain them in my home!

(Scripture verses are taken from Holy Bible, New Living Translation, copyright 1996, 2004, 2015 by Tyndale House Foundation.)

Becky Davis – OOG Leader

From being a student to a kitchen helper, then a leader, this ministry is one of the richest ministries I have encountered. The Biblical teaching is spot on! It refined, convicted, challenged, and shaped my heart to be a better wife, mom, friend, and woman. I so appreciated the women leaders who poured into us and shared their hearts so authentically to help us grow.

Jenny Curtiss – Wife to Ben 15 years, Mom
to three amazing boys (ages 5, 8 and 11)

When I was first married, I could not cook anything! OOG gave me the confidence to start making more homemade meals . . . but also grew me in my faith. Many years later, I was able to host, cook, and mentor women in their faith. I love this beautiful cycle of discipleship.

Carlie Cope – OOG Participant and Mentor

Ornaments of Grace has been a most fulfilling ministry for me as mentor in several classes. As an older woman, this has given me inspiration as I have come to know and encourage many younger women striving to live out their roles in a godly manner.

Tammy McClintic – Teaching Director for Community Bible Study, Eternally Adored Child of God

Introduction

Ornaments of Grace is a Titus 2 mentoring ministry. Its name is derived from *Proverbs 3:21, 22 (NIV) – ". . . preserve sound judgment and discernment, do not let them out of your sight; they will be life for you, an ornament to grace your neck."*

The *Ornaments of Grace* curriculum is based foundationally on *Titus 2:1, 3-5 (ESV) "But as for you, teach what accords with sound doctrine. Older women likewise are to be reverent in behavior, not slanderers or slaves to much wine. They are to teach what is good, and so train the young women to love their husbands and children, to be self-controlled, pure, working at home, kind and submissive to their own husbands, that the word of God may not be reviled."*

It is generally accepted that the Apostle Paul was the author of the pastoral letter books of 1 and 2 Timothy and Titus. These letters provide instruction and guidance from Paul to these pastors. After Paul's imprisonment in Rome (A.D. 60-62), he began his fourth missionary journey, during which he commissioned Titus to remain in Crete and Timothy in Ephesus.[1]

Titus was a Gentile (Greek) convert of Paul who had assisted him in his ministry in Ephesus during his third missionary journey. From there, Paul sent Titus to Corinth

---

[1]

to help with the church. Titus then worked with Paul in Crete next and was commissioned by Paul to remain there as his representative. The book of Titus is one of the letters Paul wrote to Titus to guide and encourage him as he pastored the people there. Life at this time in Crete had sunk to a deplorable moral level, proverbially characterized by its dishonesty, gluttony and laziness (1:12).

The direction given to us by Paul's teachings wisely show how women can grow in wisdom and their knowledge of God through strong relationships, being deliberate in our actions and by example. The *Ornaments of Grace* ministry seeks to provide a way for women to see how God's word impacts their families and homes in a practical application. The ministry focuses on women's growth through relationship and example, through a practical application of meal preparation, sharing the meal together, and topically studying God's word as it related to family. In addition to Paul's words in Titus, additional scripture is included topically from a variety of subjects that are to be taught to younger women by the word and example of older women.

The references used to prepare this Introduction were:
The NIV Study Bible; copyright 1985 by The Zondervan Corporation
The New Spirit Filled Life Bible, NLT version; copyright 2013 by Thomas Nelson, Inc.

All scriptures within the following materials (Lessons 1 through 6) are taken from the English Standard Version, unless otherwise noted; Copyright 2001 by Crossway, a publishing ministry of Good News Publishers.

Lesson 1, Part 1: Preparing for Mentoring

Please note that all scripture references are from the ESV unless noted otherwise.

Titus 2:1, 3- 5 – "But as for you, teach what accords with sound doctrine. Older women likewise are to be reverent in behavior, not slanderers or slaves to much wine. They are to teach what is good, and so train the young women to love their husbands and children, to be self-controlled, pure, working at home, kind and submissive to their own husbands, that the word of God may not be reviled."

God intends for us to regard every part of life as holy and to live out our various callings in such a godly way to bring honor and glory to God. Failure to do so would cause the word of God to be reviled by non-believers. (See also Titus 2: 8, 10)

Question 1

Older women are commanded here in Titus to instruct younger women in what is good, both by word and by example. The Greek word used here for train is "sophronizo" which means to train, encourage, advise. Why do you think God commands the teaching of sound doctrine via the method of mentoring?

Question 2

Who were some of your key role models in your youth, and how did they influence you?

Question 3

Why do you think it is sometimes difficult to find willing mentors in the church today? How might you go about finding mentors, and what are your expectations of those relationships?

Question 4

Which quality in Titus 2: 4, 5 seems most important to you and why? Most difficult?

Question 5

"Working at home" may seem like a less spiritual endeavor than the others, but it is an equally important ministry to us as wives and mothers. We sometimes adopt our culture's thinking that the sacred and the secular are separate parts of our lives. God is in us and with us at all times and in all we think, feel, do and say! In light of Colossians 3:23, what do you think it means to be working at home? How would you assess the value of this work? (Please note that we do not believe this means that a woman may not work outside the home also. This is a matter to be decided prayerfully by a woman and her husband. But even if she does work outside, she must still maintain a priority of managing the work of the home.)

An important area we will teach during each of our mentoring classes is food preparation and presentation. The dinner table is an important and all but lost tradition in the home today. In fact, Italians regard family dinner time so highly that they refer to it as "The Sacred Table".

God placed much significance upon feasting for celebrations in the Old Testament as well as breaking bread in Christian fellowship in the New Testament. In fact, He must even enjoy cooking; listen to what He says in Isaiah 25:6 . . . *"On this mountain the Lord of hosts will make for all peoples a feast of rich food, a feast of well-aged wine, of rich food full of marrow, of aged wine well refined . . ."*

Question 6

Given the busyness of our lives, how are you establishing the habit of honoring the family dinner table in your home? What might you do differently?

Question 7

During our six sessions together, we hope to inspire you to experience real joy in cooking and ministering to your family in all the Titus II principles. What do you hope to learn or accomplish by the completion of this course?

Lesson 1, Part 2: Kindness

Titus 2:1, 3-5 – ". . . train the younger women to be kind . . ."

Question 1

Look in your dictionary and compare the definitions of "kind" and "nice". What does each of these mean and how do they differ?

Question 2

God commands us to be kind because He is kind (Ephesians 2:7). Also God gives us some compelling reasons in scripture to be kind. (See Ephesians 4: 31, 32.) What are some reasons for and benefits of kindness?

Question 3

God commands us to be kind, and He forms that trait within us, through the guidance of the Holy Spirit (Galatians 5: 16-24). Our human nature makes it easier to be kind to some people than to others. According to each of the verses below, to whom must we show kindness? (Note: the terms "kindness" and "generous" are substituted for one another in various translations of the Bible.)

Proverbs 14: 21, 31
Proverbs 19:17
Daniel 4:27
Luke 6:35
I Thessolonians 5:15
2 Timothy 2:24

What are some specific ways in which you can show kindness to each of these groups?

Question 4

It is easy to take the family for granted and to neglect showing kindness in the home, particularly in tone of voice. How are you doing in this area, and what changes might you need to make? (Refer to I Corinthians 13 and Colossians 3:12-14)

Question 5

You might feel that it just isn't in your nature to be kind. Since each of us was born with a sin nature, most of what feels "natural" to us is sinful. God commands us to fight this fleshly battle and to put on His nature. (Colossians 3: 5-17). What specific actions can you take in order to "clothe yourself with kindness"?

Question 6

Random House defines kind as "of a good or benevolent nature" and nice as "pleasing, agreeable, and delightful". When might confronting someone be the kindest thing you can do, even if the person does not think you are being nice? (Psalm 141:5)

Question 7

Sometimes a confrontation is necessary with another person.

Read the following passages, and then note the principles and steps you find which would help you to handle a confrontation in a biblically appropriate manner. (Matthew 5:24, 25 and Luke 17:3, 4)

Question 8

Have you ever been the recipient of an undeserved kindness; if so, how?

Question 9

What change(s) will you make as a result of reflecting on God's words regarding kindness?

Lesson 2:
Working at Home

Titus 2:1, 3-5 – ". . . working at home . . ."

The Greek word, *oikurgos,* used in this "working at home" mandate refers to domestic matters. Bruce's commentary suggests that a woman's directive to be busy at home suggests that this is the woman's main sphere (The International Bible Commentary by F. F. Bruce, Published 1986, p. 1494).

The mere mention of the word "homemaking" among a diverse group of women can arouse the false divide of the largely secularly imposed "mommy wars". The "wife of noble character" (praised in Proverbs 31) might represent any godly woman with her multi-faceted life of service. She is quite accomplished in both domestic and commercial endeavors and still has time for helping others outside of the family. While this account may indeed be a panoramic sweep of her life over time, it is interesting to note that there is not a hint of conflict mentioned in this scripture between her and her contemporaries.

A woman's decision to work outside the home should be carefully made under the auspices of scripture and prayer and in submission to the husband's needs and desires. In either case, whether she works outside the home or not, she must still tend to her domestic responsibilities. We believe a good guide for a wife/mother to use to order her priorities is: God first, husband second, children third, work fourth, church/outside activities fifth, all with prayerful consideration and appropriate attention to self care.

Question 1

Read Proverbs 31:10-31. What do you admire most about "a woman who fears the Lord" (Or "the wife of noble character" in the NIV)? What intimidates you about her?

Question 2

Read Matthew 20:26, Galatians 5:13, Ephesians 6:7, Philippians 2:6-11. How does an understanding of God's character encourage a life of humility and service in us?

Question 3

Being well-organized is foundational to making our homemaking productive and efficient. You will need to regularly re-evaluate your organizational systems and methods to determine if they are working effectively for you and your family. Complete the **"Getting Organized Self-Questionnaire" (Addendum 1** at the end of this lesson).

The Self-Questionnaire can serve as a guide for where you need to focus in getting yourself properly organized at home. Much good material abounds on this topic at your local bookstore. What key self-discovery did you find after completing the Questionnaire?

Question 4

God's word has much to say about how we use our time. He also tells us how we often waste it, such as in . . .

Worrying (Luke 11:3, Luke 12:25, 26)
Idleness (Titus 2:4, 5)
Gossip (Proverbs 13:3)
Minding Other People's Business (I Thessalonians 4:11)
Poor Planning (Proverbs 15:22)

Which of these areas presents the greatest problem for you, and what will you do about it?

Question 5

How would you describe your housekeeping habits? Ask your husband to answer this same question for you (how he views your housekeeping). What discrepancies did you find between these two points of view (if any), and what changes could you make to create a more comfortable and pleasing home environment? How might you and your husband better share the responsibilities of the home?

The key areas which will occupy your work at home include doing laundry, mending, cleaning, budgeting and paying bills, meal planning and cooking, shopping and running errands. These topics are far too vast for us to cover in this lesson, but are important matters for you to master. You can find helpful books by such authors as Emilie Barnes, Don Aslett, or websites like The Fly Lady, Organizing Made Fun, Clean & Scentsible, I Heart Organizing, Organizing Home Life, Unclutterer and other home management experts. There are also organizational apps available for your smartphone like Evernote.

A sampling of materials is included along with this lesson for further information, including:

Advice From a Fellow Student by
Leisa Ress (Addendum 2)
Meal Planning & Grocery Shopping (Addendum 3)

Question 6

Another ministry of the home is offering hospitality to others, friends and even to strangers. Read Deuteronomy 10:18-19, Romans 12:13 and 16:23, Hebrews 13:1-2, I Peter 4:9, I John 3:17-18 and Revelation 3:20. In light of these scriptures, to whom might you show hospitality and how might you do this? Refer also to *"Thoughts Regarding Hospitality" by Barb Duncan (Addendum 4).*

Question 7

Read I Timothy 3:2 and Titus 1:8; do you think from these verses that God requires men also to show hospitality? How can you and your husband minister together in this area?

Question 8

Aesthetics matter in your home. God created us with an eye for beauty, as He surveyed His own creation and evaluated it as "good". What part of God's amazing creation takes your breath away, and describe how you feel when you observe or experience it?

Question 9

How is God's appreciation for beauty reflected in the atmosphere of your home? In artwork and décor? In the use of lighting (including candlelight) and music to create an aesthetically pleasing environment? Your home should be your castle—for both you and your husband; this calls for an atmosphere of peace and tranquility, insulating you from the battles fought outside in the world all day. (See Proverbs 21:9.)

Question 10

Not everyone is a gifted decorator, and certainly most of us do not have a lavish budget for these things. Even so, each of us can use our imaginations and creativity to make the most of the aesthetics in our own homes. What changes could you make to enhance the beauty and comfort of your domain?

For Further Reading

Allie Casazza has an absolutely fabulous podcast and website
(alliecasazza.com)

What's A Smart Woman Like You Doing at Home by Burton,
Dittmer and *Loveless*

Home by Choice by Brenda Hunter, Ph.D.

Should You be the Working Mom by Bee-Lang C. Wang,
Ph.D.

Mary Whelchel's works and website to help
Christian women who work outside the home
(Christianworkingwoman.org).

The Nesting Place by Myquillyn Smith

Addendum 1 - Getting Organized Self-Questionnaire

1. My Life Purpose in one sentence would be:

2. My expectations of how I use my time are:

3. My husband expects the following of me:

4. How do the above sets of expectations contribute to the overall accomplishment of my Life Purpose and the priorities which flow from it?

5. What activities am I currently doing on a regular basis which do not contribute to the accomplishment of my Life Purpose?

6. How do I currently keep track of appointments, commitments and tasks to be done each day?

7. What previous attempts have I made at getting organized? Have they been successful, and why or why not?

8. How often do I find myself regretting commitments I've made for my time? Do I wait to give a "yes" answer to requests for my time and pray first?

9. Do I have regular blocks of time each week which are reserved for household responsibilities, and during which I try to refuse invitations or requests for other uses of my time?

10. Am I willing to commit to a minimum of 15 minutes of time per week in which to plan out my next week?

Addendum 2 - Advice From a Fellow Student of Homemaking

By Leisa Ress

<u>Make time with God in His Word and prayer your top priority.</u> As a bonus, you will find that the rest of your day will be better and you will be more equipped to handle problems that arise.

<u>Keep a calendar – a bare minimum must do!</u> Find whatever kind you like and what works for you. Record all of your appointments and commitments on it and plan your week from it. Stay focused on the task at hand. Live in the present moment. (Very difficult for me!) From your monthly calendar, make a Daily sheet for each day of the upcoming week; include "To Do", "Appointments", and "Administration/Communication".

For <u>tasks on which you find yourself procrastinating,</u> try the <u>"I'll give it 15 minutes"</u> approach. Set a timer and work for 15 minutes on the undesirable task. Often just getting started is the problem. You might find yourself deciding to keep on working until the job is completed. At least you will have accomplished a good portion of it.

Find methods to minimize clutter.

Open mail by a garbage can and throw away each piece of paper you can.

Immediately file the papers you *must* keep in their proper places. If it can be retrieved electronically later from your email or on line, don't keep a hard copy.

Have an office set up (can be in a closet or desk in kitchen) where you have everything you need for paying bills, balancing your checkbook, etc. Paying bills on line saves a lot of time and keeps past payment information easy to retrieve.

Use your reminder function on your smartphone to keep you on top of upcoming responsibilities.

Do a 15-minute run-though the house each day, tossing items in a bag which you can throw away or donate until the clutter has been greatly reduced in your home. (The Fly Lady's idea) Create zones for yourself and other family members in which to put items that otherwise result in excess clutter. Put things away as you go.

Label storage boxes with description of contents. Also, label leftovers stored in refrigerator.

Keep a master Household Organization & Planning binder with sections pertinent to your needs. These might include Holidays, Gift Shopping, Warranties, Travel, Activities, etc.

Keep cleaning supplies and rags in each bathroom (out of sight and reach of the children, of course!), and clean as you go. Also, keep used grocery bags in bathrooms for emptying garbage cans.

To simplify laundry, keep a few tall kitchen garbage cans, each marked with the type of load. Automatically sort as you throw dirty clothes in baskets. When a basket is nearly full, you have an already sorted load to wash.

Keep toy baskets in rooms where you and your children spend a lot of time.

Develop a 15-Minute Spruce-Up plan which you can do (and involve your children) just before your husband comes home. Perfection is not the goal; it is the enemy of the good enough. *"Each one of us can live such a life of amazing power and peace and serenity, of integration and confidence and simplified multiplicity, on one condition – that is, if we really want to."* – Thomas Kelly

Addendum 3- Meal Planning & Grocery Shopping

The Weekly Meal Planning/ Grocery Shopping Session Materials

Set aside a block of time once each week in which you will plan your meals for the following week and write a grocery shopping list. These are the elements you will want to consider:

Current grocery store flyer (via mail or on line).

Your coupons (collected via the Sunday paper inserts, internet, etc.)

Your **Meal Planning Recipe List**

Your file of **"New Recipes to Try"** which you have collected from magazines, Food Network, recipe websites, friends, etc.

Your master **"Shopping Needs List"** (explained later)

Meal Planning Recipe List

Keep a list of the recipes you use, either by hand on 3X5 cards, or in your computer, organized by food category (i.e. beef, chicken, salads, soups, desserts, pasta, etc.). Each category names the specific recipes and the cookbook in which you can find it. You can easily update this list on an on-going basis. When you try a new recipe, you will either decide to add it to your recipe list or forget it if the family didn't like it.

Master Grocery Shopping List

Keep a sheet of paper in an easily accessible place to all the family. I add to this list throughout the week any items I notice we are low on. I also expect each family member to list items they want. That way, no one can complain when an item is out of stock—it's their job too! I will admit that when my kids were very young, I would often find largely scrawled letters for items such as "candy", "ice cream", etc. You'll be combining this list with your needed ingredients each week to plan your grocery shopping trip.

Making Your Week's Meal Plan

List the items you want to plan around given the store sales and your existing freezer and pantry inventory.

Given this input, list the meals you want to prepare for the following week; for example, I plan on cooking six nights per week. I lay out six dinners, varying the types of meat/meatless dishes I want to prepare. Then I try to vary the degree of difficulty, so that I am making a few challenging recipes (and usually one or two new ones), but am also making some quick and easy dinners for the nights I will be busier otherwise.

After I determine the six main dishes I'll serve, I pick

side dishes for each from my recipe cards and new recipes file. On this 6 night meal plan list, I note the cookbook in which I will find each of the selected recipes.

Next I get out all of those cookbooks and list the ingredients needed for those recipes. If possible, I scale down the amount I'll need given my family is not big on left-overs. I check this list against my existing inventory and add to my general grocery shopping list those items I will need to purchase.

Next I pull any coupons which might apply, noting the requirements on my shopping list (i.e. 2 boxes of 3 oz. Jell-O Gelatin)

Then I add to my shopping lists any additional really good sale items which I might not need for that week, but could be inventoried for future use.

I also do some bulk buying at Sam's Club and Costco, but know your prices! Some items can actually be cheaper at the regular grocery store when they are featured loss leaders.

Then I lay out my final grocery shopping list. I list the items by category in order of the store layout. You can often obtain a store map from your grocery or on line. This saves back-tracing time and steers me directly to the sections I need to shop, helping me to avoid those extra impulse purchases.

Keeping Your Grocery Bill Lower

Don't shop when you are hungry; you are more susceptible to being enticed by impulse purchases.

Shop only the sections which have the items on your list.

Stick to your list, unless you discover a really great sale on something which you might want to back stock.

Do home-made foods as much as possible; avoid pre-packaged convenience foods. This is not a religious mandate; however, there are times when the excess cost is worth it for the time you will save and use for better purposes.

Some of My Favorite Recipe Sources

Friends and family
Southern Living Magazine
Cooks Illustrated Magazine
Eating Well Magazine
Food Network (on line at Foodnetwork.com)
Fine Cooking on line
Ina Garten & Ree Drummond (The Pioneer Woman)

Addendum 4 - Thoughts Regarding Hospitality

By Barb Duncan

There is a difference between showing hospitality and entertaining. A detriment to hospitality is pride.

Showing hospitality isn't always convenient.

Good manners means making other people feel comfortable.

Budget to practice hospitality.

Sharing a meal with others in an intimate occasion…it is a covenant practice.

"Christ is the Head of this house, the unseen guest at every meal, the silent listener to every conversation."

Keep an extra frozen dessert of some type in the freezer for unexpected company, or to take over when invited for an impromptu dinner.

When inviting guests, pray over the selection of guests. Inquire about dietary needs, preferences or allergies. Consider the menu, setting, and situation to accommodate the comfort level of your guests, keeping their possible desire of reciprocation in mind.

Keep their next day's schedule in mind regarding the length and timing of the event.

Involve your children if possible.

When having overnight guests, stock up on toiletries – toothbrushes, mini-deodorants, shampoos and soaps – at the dollar store. Keep in a basket labeled, "Guests, please help yourselves!" Have clean towels and wash cloths out and readily available to guests.

Keep some convenience items in easy sight in your guest room (e.g. water pitcher and glasses, small chocolates, paper and pen, simple alarm clock, reading material, night light.)

When you are a guest, be a gracious receiver
of hospitality as well as a giver. Teach your
children to be good guests also.

When your children are teenagers and tell you they
are invited to be a guests at a party, get the phone
number of their host and call, asking if you can send
a couple of bottles of soda along with your child. In
this way, you are not only participating in hospitality,
but also find out if there is really a party (with parent's
knowledge.) No phone number of host? NO party!

Leisa Ress

Leisa Ress

Leisa Ress

Leisa Ress

Leisa Ress

Leisa Ress

Lesson 3:
Loving Your Husband

Titus 2:1, 3-5, – ". . .Then they can train the younger women to love their husbands."

Titus 2 admonishes the older women to teach the younger women "to love their husbands". If love can be taught and learned, then it must be more than a "feeling", as being "in love" would suggest. Look at I Corinthians 13: 1-3, 13 and see what exceedingly great emphasis God places on love. God regards love as a higher calling than even "faith that can move mountains".

God Himself is not just "loving", but He *is* love. (I John 4: 8, 16) Is it any wonder that He regards love as the greatest of Christian virtues? He made the supreme sacrifice of love at Calvary for us, and He expects that love to manifest itself in us through service to others, beginning with our husbands.

Of all the directives we are given to live godly lives, Jesus says loving our neighbor is our second greatest commandment. (Matthew 22:39) The closest neighbor you have is your husband. After God, he is to be your first priority.

Question 1

What are some loving actions you do for your husband?

Question 2

Read I Corinthians 13: 4-7. Does God define love here as a feeling or an action? List the manifestations of love identified here in scripture.

Question 3

You love your husband when you are patient with and kind to him. You are not envious of his accomplishments, but rejoice with him. You are not boastful, nor are your actions self-promoting and motivated by pride. You are not rude to him, nor are you easily angered. You do not keep a record of wrongs. You rejoice with the truth, seeking resolution of disagreements over winning. You always protect, trust, hope and persevere in your marriage. How are you presently doing in loving your husband, and in what areas do you need to improve?

The two primary ways in which you show love for your husband is through respect and sex. Read Ephesians 5:22-33. What are some ways you show respect for and to your husband?

What are some qualities you admire in your husband (and be sure and tell him so!)?

God has given the gift of sexual intimacy to be enjoyed only within the confines of marriage. From the very beginning of his word, He shows us that His perfect plan for a husband and wife was to unabashedly enjoy one another's bodies. See how the first married couple was naked and unashamed in Genesis 2: 4-25). Notice how God saw Adam's need for a mate and demonstrated this to him in the process of naming the animals.

We live in a fallen world which has grossly defiled God's plan for human sexuality. We are tainted by pornographic images in the media and by improper views of sex. We sometimes bring guilt from past sins in this area into our present marriage beds. Sexual sin must be repented of (even if it was premarital sex with your husband), but is just as forgivable as any other sin!

Question 4

What are some wrong messages the world gives about sex? What misconceptions have you adopted about sex?

Hebrews 13:4 says the marriage bed is to be kept undefiled. In light of this command, Christian women are sometimes prone to be confused about what is and is not appropriate in her sexual relationship with her husband. When asking oneself whether a thing is appropriate or not, a good quick list of questions to consider are: (1) Does God forbid it? (2) Does it involve a third party, either in person or visual image? (3) Is it mutually agreeable to both husband and wife?

First she must examine the scriptures to determine what God has specifically forbidden (Matthew 5:27, 28, 32; I Corinthians 6:9-20; Ephesians 5:3; Colossians 3:5; I Thessalonians 4:2-8; Hebrews 13:4). If God has forbidden it, then it is always wrong, even within marriage. This would include pornography of any type as it is impure and results in lust for wrong persons. This list of forbidden behaviors would by definition exclude anyone outside the marriage in this intimate relationship, either directly in person or indirectly via media. Otherwise, if a husband and wife enjoy expressing their love in creative ways with one another, it should be fully enjoyed without guilt. Sexual intimacy between you and your husband is God's wedding gift to you!

Question 5

What behaviors are forbidden by the scriptures above?

A couple of helpful books for women who may want to better understand men's struggles and their own with sexual purity include: *Every Man's Battle*, by Stephen Arterburn, and *Every Woman's Battle*, by Stephen Arterburn and Shannon Ethridge. For an exhaustive examination of specific questions and concerns about sex, we highly recommend the book, *Intimate Issues* by Linda Dillow and Lorraine Pintus*. This book consults scripture to answer questions like:

How can I be godly and sensuous?
How can I shift into sexual gear?
How can I get over the guilt of past sexual sin?
How can sex go from boring to sizzling?
What's not okay in bed? (The book gets very specific here!)
How can I recapture the passion?

*Linda Dillow and Dr. Juli Slattery also developed this material into a women's Bible study, called *Passion Pursuit: What Kind of Love Are You Making?*

A few other books you may want to read are *The Gift of Sex: A Guide To Sexual Fulfillment*, by Clifford and Joyce Penner, and *For Women Only* by Shaunti Feldhahn.

This next assignment will take some time, but it is critical for gaining a proper appreciation of God's plan for sexual intimacy in marriage.

Read Song of Songs (Chapters 1, 3 & 5) to see a passionate description of the intensity God intended for the sexual relationship between a husband and wife. Note also that theologians have long believed that this is also an allegory of the love relationship between Christ and the church. The sexual union of man and woman mirrors the spiritual intimacy and oneness Christ desires to have with us.

Notice how the wife in Song of Songs positively anticipates sex with her husband. She praises the things she delights in him and provocatively invites him to enjoy her body. Throughout this poetic and romantic book, observe how this wife is creative and eager in their sex life.

Question 6

Sex is in fact a marital duty (I Corinthians 7:3), but God intends it to be so much more beautiful and satisfying. The wife's body belongs also to her husband and vice versa (I Corinthians 7: 4, 5), and a partner must not withhold his or her body from the other except by mutual consent for a limited time in order to be devoted to prayer. Failure to obey this command opens the door to Satan to tempt one or both marriage partners. Why and how might a woman be inclined to misuse or avoid sex in her marriage?

Read Proverbs 5:19 (preferably in more than one version) to see how God intends you to delight your husband with your body. The ESV says: "A lovely dear, a graceful doe. Let her breasts fill you at all times with delight; be intoxicated always in her love." Spend some time in prayer today asking God to show you how you can make the sexual union all he intends for it to be for you and your husband. And get started tonight!

Lesson 4:
Loving Your Children

Titus 2:1, 3-5 – ". . .Then they can train the younger women to love their husbands and children . . ."

God has entrusted to us our children; we are to receive them as His gift and to love and raise them according to His word. Loving our children usually comes quite naturally to us.

Psalm 127:3 – "Behold, children are a heritage from the Lord, the fruit of the womb a reward."

<u>Question 1</u>

Recall the birth of your first child; what memories and feelings come to mind?

We often hear parents comment that they are raising their children to eventually become independent. Perhaps our perspective should be rather that we are raising them to eventually transfer their dependence from being upon us (their parents) to being upon God, their eternal Heavenly Father.

Proverbs 22:6 – "Train a child up in the way he should go, even when he is old he will not depart from it."

Question 2

List ways a child learns to depend upon God (1) from his relationship with you, and (2) from specific ways you teach him to do so?

Deuteronomy 6:5-7 – "You shall love the Lord your God with all your heart and with all your soul and with all your might. And these words that I command you today shall be on your heart. You shall teach them diligently to your children, and shall talk of them when you sit in your house, and when you walk by the way, and when you lie down, and when you rise."

Joel 1:3 – "Tell your children of it, and let your children tell their children, and their children to another generation." (Note how you can reach into future generations for God.)

Question 3

How can you live out these verses in training your children?

Question 4

In the lesson on "Loving Your Husband", you examined the correct order of priorities in your life: (God first, husband second, children third, while also tending to our own self care needs.) Our children are so precious that we can sometimes find it easy to love the gift above the Giver. Do you find this order difficult to keep, and if so, how can you address this?

Question 5

Have you ever considered that God chose you to parent the specific children He has given you? Read the following verses and list some reasons you believe God may have given you the children you have.

Jeremiah 1:5a – "Before I formed you in the womb I knew you, and before you were born I consecrated you;"

Acts 17:26 – "And he made from one man every nation of mankind to live on all the face of the earth, having determined allotted periods and the boundaries of their dwelling place."

Question 6

One of our most important jobs as parents is to discipline our children. Just as God disciplines us and we are blessed by it (Psalm 94:12), so are our children blessed when we properly discipline them.

Deuteronomy 32:46 – He said to them, "Take to heart all the words by which I am warning you today, so that you may command them to your children, that they may be careful to do all the words of this law."

What is the main discipline problem in your home right now? What does God say about that issue? Have you asked God for the wisdom to address this matter?

Hebrews 12:9, 10, 11 – "Besides this, we have all had earthly fathers who disciplined us and we respected them. Shall we not much more be subject to the Father of spirits and live? For they disciplined us for a short time as it seemed best to them, but he disciplines us for our good, that we may share his holiness. For the moment all discipline seems painful rather than pleasant, but later it yields the peaceful fruit of righteousness to those who have been trained by it."

Question 7

How have you personally experienced such a harvest and have you seen this result from the disciplining of your children?

Proverbs 19:18 – "Discipline your son, for there is hope; do not set your heart on putting him to death."

Question 8

How could lack of discipline result in death?

Proverbs 13:24 – "Whoever spares the rod hates his son, but he who loves him is diligent to discipline him."

Proverbs 22:15 – "Folly is bound up in the heart of a child, but the rod of discipline drives it far from him."

Proverbs 23:13, 14 – "Do not withhold discipline from a child; if you strike him with a rod, he will not die. If you strike him with the rod, you will save his soul from Sheol."

Proverbs 29:15, 17 – "The rod and reproof give wisdom, but a child left to himself brings shame to his mother. Discipline your son, and he will give you rest; he will give delight to your heart."

Question 9

Scriptures refer to the "rod of discipline" often and in a necessary and vital light. To what do you think this rod refers and how is this carried out with your children?

Discipline must be tempered with grace. The motive must be to obey God and bring honor and glory to Him in raising our children. When pride is my motive, my child will not be blessed by it, nor will God be honored. There may be times when we deem it necessary to share with one of our children a specific failure from our past; this must be done under the guidance of the Holy Spirit, considering whether such sharing will **edify** or **excuse** that very behavior in your child.

Ephesians 6:4 – "Fathers, do not provoke your children to anger, but bring them up in the discipline and instruction of the Lord."

Colossians 3:21 – "Fathers, do not provoke your children, lest they become discouraged."

Question 10

Have your ever felt exasperated or embittered by discipline you received, and what effect did it have on you?

Question 11

What methods or tactics might you need to change now in order to make sure your discipline is seasoned with grace?

Prayer should be the driving force behind our parenting. God should be the first one we run to for counsel and support. He may at times direct us to older, more experienced Christians for advice, but He remains the ultimate authority.

It is particularly effective to pray God's word for your

children. Make a list of the traits and behaviors you want to see your children have and mature into as adults. Find scriptures on these topics to pray for them.

When our children are rebellious and disobedient, we can feel like failures as parents. But children are endowed with free will and are able to exercise this throughout their entire lives, with varying degrees of consequences. The only perfect parent is God, The Father; listen to what He had to say about His rebellious children . . . *Isaiah 1:2 – "Hear, O heavens and give ear, O earth; for the Lord has spoken: "Children have I reared and brought up, but they have rebelled against me."*

Question 12

Read *Luke 15: 11-31, The Parable of the Prodigal Son.* Have you ever been the prodigal child and experienced your parents' grace? How did it feel?

Consider how you might keep your heart ready to extend grace and forgive your children when necessary.

Question 13

Read *Proverbs 31:10-31, The Woman Who Fears the Lord,* noting in particular v. 28 – "*Her children rise up and call her blessed; her husband also, and he praises her.*" If you feel overwhelmed by this woman's amazing accomplishments, keep in mind that this is a panoramic view of a woman's life. Not all was done in a day or even in a season! Meditate on the qualities you would like to exemplify in your own home and life, and note them below.

Suggestions for Further Reading:

What Happens When We Pray for Our Families by Evelyn
    Christenson
I Was a Better Mother Before I Had Kids by Lori Borgman
Pass the Faith by Lori Borgman
The Five Love Languages of Children by Gary Chapman
Boundaries with Kids by Henry Cloud and John Townsend
Shepherding a Child's Heart by Tedd Tripp
Bringing up Boys by James Dobson
Wild at Heart by John Eldredge
What's a Smart Women Like You Doing at Home by Burton,
    Dittmer and Loveless
The Power of a Praying Parent by Stormie Omartian
Say Goodbye to Whining by Scott Turansky and Joanne
    Miller
Dare to Discipline by James Dobson
Creative Correction by Lisa Whelchel
Parenting With Love and Logic by Foster Cline
Have a New Kid by Friday by Kevin Leman
Finding Your Purpose as a Mom by Donna Otto
You Can't Make Me, But I Can Be Persuaded by Cynthia
    Tobias
*The Connected Child: Bring Hope and helaing to Your Adoptive
Family* by Karyn B. Purvis, David R. Cross, and Wendy
    Sunshine
Also for children from particularly difficult places (abuse,
    neglect, trauma), see the method, Trust Based
    Relational Intervention (TBRI) by Dr. Karyn B.
    Purvis on the website child.tcu.edu

Lesson 5:
Marital Submission

Titus 2:1, 3-5 – ". . . and to be submissive to their own husbands . . ."

Our modern culture views the concept of a wife being submissive to her husband as altogether passé. Many women today consider themselves to be liberated from such antiquated thinking and completely equal to their husbands in authority within the marriage. But God's perfect plan for marriage and family does establish an order of authority, with the husband as its head (in submission to God), and parents in authority over their children.

To be *subject to* in the Greek is the word, *hypotasso,* which means to put in subjection, subject, subordinate, to submit to be subject to. It is a voluntary act to submit to the husband's authority in leadership, a decision of the heart. (Titus 2:5 tells the older women to teach the younger women to do this act of the will.)

Question 1

What thoughts and feelings come to mind as you consider this imperative to submit to your husband, and why can submission be so difficult for us?

God has assigned to the husband the position of leadership in the home, and has required of him a sacrificial love for his wife.

Ephesians 5:22-25 – "Wives, submit to your own husbands, as to the Lord. For the husband is the head of the wife even as Christ is the head of the church, His body, and is Himself its Savior. Now as the church submits to Christ, so also wives should submit in everything to their husbands. Husbands, love your wives, as Christ loved the church and gave Himself up for her."

Question 2

What does it mean for a husband to love his wife as Christ loved the church? How does this scripture help you more willingly submit to your husband?

Question 3

The above scripture says that wives must submit to their husbands *"in everything"*. Is there ever a time when a wife would be justified in not submitting to her husband? Read Acts 5:1-11 and Acts 5:29 as you ponder this question.

It has been said that the biblical mandate for a wife is *complete submission without personal sin*. In the case above, Sapphira submitted to her husband by following his example of lying. She was admonished by Peter for doing so and was struck dead just as her husband had been.

Question 4

Having examined this exception to the rule of submission, how might a wife be tempted to use this as an excuse to unjustifiably defy her husband's authority?

Sadly there are times when a husband goes to the extreme of inflicting serious abuse upon his wife, either emotionally or physically. A woman must remove herself (and children) from any real threat of harm. She must be careful not to use this as a loophole to leave a difficult marriage however.

I Corinthians 7:10 says that *"a wife should not separate from her husband."*

In the opinion of James D. Craig, PhD, LMFT (Northern Light Christian Counseling, Indianapolis) "verbal abuse" is a pervasive pattern of threatening words and behavior that suggests imminent violence. Dr. Craig points out that Jesus himself said, "Out of the abundance of the heart, the mouth speaks." Verbal abuse indicated a person's intent to harm one's spouse and is therefore a fundamental violation of the marital vows "to love, honor, and cherish."

Dr. Craig further says that contrary to what is often taught, Jesus did not hold adultery to be the only legitimate ground for divorce. For example, in Matthew 5:32, Jesus uses the word *"pornea"* (where we get our words *"pornography"* and *"fornication"*) as the ground for divorce. This word encompasses all sorts of sexual sin, not just adultery.

In such circumstances, the wife is wise to prayerfully seek the advice of a trusted mentor or Christian counselor to be sure she is acting within biblical reason.

Question 5

Sometimes a wife must suffer the injustice of submitting to a husband who is not behaving in a Christ like manner toward her (either because he is not a Christian, or because he is a Christian living in disobedience.) Does God require a wife to remain in submission to her husband in these situations? (Consider I Peter 3:1-6 in answering, and please note that as addressed before, this is **not** referring to cases of actual abuse.)

Question 6

When a wife willingly submits, for the sake of Christ, to an ungodly husband, God can use this to bring blessing to her and to others.

Romans 8:28 – "And we know that for those who love God, all things work together for good."

I Peter 3:17 – "For it is better to suffer for doing good, if that should be God's will, than for doing evil."

I Peter 4:14 – "If you are insulted for the name of Christ, you are blessed, because the Spirit of glory and of God rests upon you."

Can you think of ways that God might use a wife's suffering to bring good to her or to others?

Question 7

In Ephesians 5:33b God commands, *"and let the wife see that she respects her husband"*. The husband has a strong need to be respected by his wife, both privately and publicly.

How do you show respect for your husband, and are there ways you might be showing him disrespect? What does it do for your husband when you do respect him?

You might be thinking it is easy to submit to your husband when his decisions are "right" (in other words, when he agrees with you). But consider the idea that submission really only begins, or has relevance, when there is a collision of your wills. Otherwise it is just coincidental agreement. You are required to submit to him *"in everything"*. When you disagree with him, you must decide to arrange yourself under his authority as an act of the will.

Question 8

Being submissive does not mean being a doormat. God created Eve to be a *"helper fit"* for Adam. (Genesis 2:18)

Helper ("ezer" in Hebrew) is "one who supplies strength in the area that is lacking in: the helped." The term does not imply that the helper is either stronger or weaker than the one helped. A wife is not her husband's clone but complements him." (*ESV Study Bible footnote*)

How else can we see in scripture that "Helper" does not

imply lesser? Read John 14:15. In this verse, to whom is God referring to as "Helper"? What does this tell you?

God expects you to use your gifts and talents to suitably help your husband. How can you constructively contribute to his decision making and leadership of the family?

Question 9

Defying the authority of your husband is actually rebelling against God Himself.

Romans 13:2 – "Therefore whoever resists the authorities resists what God has appointed, and those who resist will incur judgment."

In what areas do you have difficulty submitting to your husband, and how might you be suffering consequences for your rebelliousness?

Question 10

It is God's job to perfect your husband, and your husband must answer to God for any wrong decisions he makes in the leadership of his family. God blesses obedience. Can you think of ways you and your children are blessed by your submission to God's plan for order of authority in the home?

Suggestions for Further Reading

Creative Counterpart by Linda Dillow
Becoming a Woman of Excellence by Cynthia Heald
The Power of a Praying Wife by Stormie Omartian
Love is a Decision by Gary Smalley
Adorned by Nancy DeMoss Wolegmuth
Fit to be Tied by Bill Hybels
Verbal Abuse by Patricia Evans

Lesson 6:
Self-Controlled and Pure

Titus 2:1, 3-5 – ". . . to be self-controlled and pure . . ."

The Random House English Dictionary defines self-control as the restraint of one's actions, feelings, emotions, etc. It is a fruit of the Spirit (Galatians 5:23), produced in us by God as we walk in response to the urgings of the Holy Spirit within us.

Pure is defined by the dictionary as untainted with evil or guilt, physically chaste. The Greek word used in the Bible for pure is "hagnos", meaning pure or innocent.

Self-control and purity are matters of the heart. Jesus condemned the focus on external purity while neglecting internal purity and wholeness. (Mark 7: 1-23) Self-control also involves the mind; the thoughts we think affect our level of self-control. (I Peter 1:13, 4:7, 5:8.)

It is Jesus Christ who cleanses believers from all sin (Ephesians 5:25, 26, I John 1:7.) He expects and enables us to be pure in heart. (Matthew 5:8, I Timothy 1:5)

Question 1

Read I Corinthians 9:24-27 and Romans 8:1-17. Based on these passages of Scripture, how can you live a self-controlled and pure life?

Question 2

How does your practice of the spiritual disciplines of prayer and Bible study impact your ability to live a self-controlled and pure life? Can you share examples of both ends of the spectrum, when you have been particularly blessed and when you have suffered consequences from neglect of these disciplines?

Question 3

As Christians we have much freedom to do as we please so long as it is not forbidden by God. Traders Point Christian Church (Indianapolis) Lead Pastor, Aaron Brockett, suggests that when we are determining whether or not to engage in a certain activity, we should not simply ask ourselves whether it is "okay" for us to do so, but rather if it is "best".

Read Romans 14:1-23 and I Corinthians 10:23, 24, 31. What help does this give you in making decisions about your personal freedoms as a Christian?

Question 4

How does the mandate to be self-controlled and pure apply to your words and tone of voice in the home? Refer to these passages as you consider this: Proverbs 10:19, 12:25, 15:1, 16:24, 25:11, Matthew 12:36.

Question 5

In today's culture (and sadly even in the contemporary church), we are encouraged to live life at a nearly frenetic pace. We are expected to be in many activities and to have our children in even more. We have a finite amount of time and energy and God expects us to balance our work, rest and recreation. He tells us in Genesis that we were created in part to work, and He has prepared works in advance for us to do. How can you fulfill God's purpose for yourself and still live a life which has a greater focus on "being" than on "doing", on relationships more than on activities?

Question 6

God both demonstrated and commanded a Sabbath rest from work for us. (Genesis 2:2, Exodus 20:8) How are you honoring the Sabbath? What might be hindering you from obedience to this command, and how could you change that?

Gather any group of women together for a long enough visit, and the conversation will eventually turn to our struggles to stay in shape. Generally this is a self-control issue with food and exercise. A wise pastor once said, while preaching to his congregation on marriage, "Wives, I know that man looks at the outward appearance while God looks at the heart", (I Samuel 16:7), but your husband is NOT God"! Notice that it was Rachel whom Jacob fell in love with; the Bible describes her as "lovely in form and beautiful." (Genesis 29:17) The objective is not to try to be super-models, but it is important that we try to do our best to maintain physical health and attractiveness to our husbands. We should honor our bodies as God's temples on earth.

Question 7

Read I Timothy 4: 1-16. How does this passage apply to your eating and how might you accomplish this?

Question 8

God demands sexual purity from His people. (See Matthew 15:19, I Corinthians 6:13, 18, 10:8, Galatians 5:19, Ephesians 5:3, Hebrews 13:4) He also commands wives and husbands not to deprive each other sexually, except for mutual consent for a time to be devoted to prayer, and then to come together to avoid falling due to lack of self-control. What are some subtle and insidious ways in which a marriage can be defiled by sexual impurity, and how might you guard against those?

Question 9

Read Ecclesiastes 5:10, Matthew 6:21, 2 Cor. 9:7-8, I Timothy 6:17-19, Hebrews 13:5.

How do these scriptures relate to practicing self-control in your finances?

Question 10

You may feel like you have "blown it" in the areas of purity and self-control. You might even be experiencing consequences for your negligence in these areas. But take heart; God only disciplines those He loves and for our own good (Hebrews 12:1-13). You can decide to repent today, and receive God's complete forgiveness and cleansing. (I John 1:9) Take some time now to examine yourself in these matters in prayer and listen for God's gentle guidance on what actions you might need to take.

Closing Remarks to *Ornaments of Grace* Students

We hope you have been inspired by the study of God's words to wives and mothers and encouraged by the conversations in the class.

There yet remains much to be learned in the living out of these truths. Do remain prayerful for and open to a variety of women God will place in your path as you engage in community. Also be sensitive to where God may be wanting you to speak into a younger woman's life who needs to benefit from your experience. Mentoring is really a two way street throughout life.

It is unlikely that one woman will fulfill all your mentoring needs. But a community of mentors will offer a variety of special gifts and abilities. And be sensitive to women younger than yourself who may benefit from your experiences. Mentoring is a thing to be received and given throughout life.

We leave you with this blessing from the greatest mentor, God Himself:

> *"I will instruct you and teach you in the way you should go:*
> *I will counsel you with my loving eye on you."*
> *(Psalm 32:8, NIV Study Bible; copyright 1985 by The Zondervan Corporation)*

Helps for *Ornaments of Grace* Class Leaders

More than a Bible study, this class provides for older, more experienced women to mentor younger women through 6 weekly classes. Our model is for a class last to 2 ½ hours, hosted in the home of one of the mentors. Each class is divided into three parts: a cooking demonstration, a shared meal, a discussion of the lesson for that week.

Our OOG Ministry Team also offers an on-going e-mailing of new recipes to our graduates, who regularly receive new recipes we have tested on our own families!

Because registration is very limited and a waiting list is anticipated, we require a commitment to regular attendance. We do not provide child care at the sessions. There is a modest fee for the entire six week program to partially cover food and materials.

Please visit our website for more detailed information and free helpful planning tool downloads. (ornamentsofgrace.org)

Acknowledgements

Tammy McClintic has been my rock of support since we began working in the mentoring ministry together fourteen years ago. She has been a constant source of encouragement and wisdom. She has blessed the students and other mentors so much with her gifts of hospitality and teaching. Thank you, Tammy, from the bottom of my heart!

Caroline Gilchrist has been the energizing force behind the ministry. Her enthusiasm, great ideas, and strong leadership have so inspired me. Thank you, Caroline, my dear friend!

Martha Brammer has so blessed me and the ministry with her beautiful artistry (she designed the logo among other things) and her wise and generous sharing from her life experiences as wife and mother. Thank you so much, Martha, for your grace to me and for all you have taught me.

Many thanks also to the entire *Ornaments of Grace* Ministry Team members who have prayed faithfully for the ministry, hosted classes, prepared dishes, and shared their lives with the young women and with me. Without your support and dedication, OOG would not have been sustainable.

And with deep affection, I want to thank my husband, Fred Ress, for supporting me emotionally, being so generous financially, and for being so patient with the time this ministry has required of me. Thank you, Fred, for how you have blessed me and all the *Ornaments of Grace* participants.

Author's Bio

I was blessed to grow up in a loving Christian family, very involved in our small-town church. It was there I learned the beloved Bible stories via the highest tech medium available in the 1960's, the flannel board. My school years were filled with Christian community through family and youth group events.

In college I found myself weary from a long, unsuccessful run at salvation by works. I knew that I had been forgiven of my sin upon accepting Christ at age 10, but thought it was up to me then to maintain my salvation by self-effort. It wasn't long before busyness provided all the distraction I needed to drift from the faith—obtaining my Business Administration degree, getting married, then climbing the corporate ladder in Sales and Marketing for twelve years. I knew something was missing in my life, especially contrasted to the peace and contentment I observed in my sister who had remained close to God, but I continued pursuing the accolades of my own little career god.

Becoming a mother was to heighten the dissonance between what I knew to be true and how I was living. A return to more consistent church attendance led to my searching for answers through prayer and the Word. The Holy Spirit opened my eyes to see the magnificence of the gospel of grace. He showed me how I had been forgiven of

ALL my sin – past, present, and future – and was eternally saved. None of this was by any works I had done. It was all grace, a free gift purchased for me by the death and resurrection of Jesus Christ. He made me see how my career had become my god. I did not yet know that this was merely one of a plurality of lesser gods with which I would do battle to this day. From that moment forward, I have not been able to get enough of the Word.

I have served in various capacities within the church – Sunday school teacher, food team member, Women's Ministry Leader, Discussion Leader in Bible Study Fellowship and other women's Bible studies, MOPS Mentor Mom, and for the past 14 years, Director of the mentoring ministry.

I live in Indianapolis, Indiana, with my husband of 39 years, Fred. We have two adult children, Meredith Walton and Evan Ress. Meredith and her husband, John, have given us three beautiful grandchildren-Cate, Paul, and Claire. Evan and his lovely wife, Cassy, have given us two lovable grand dogs, Leo and Artie.

Printed in the United States
By Bookmasters